AUSTRALIA

a visual journey across an island continent

Middle Harbour looking towards
Grotto Point, Sydney

AUSTRALIA
A visual journey across an island continent

Design Aron Vella / Darren Holt
Editor Aron Vella / Dan Hormillosa

Printed in China through Colorcraft Ltd., Hong Kong

ISBN 1-86315-246-6

Little Hills Press Pty. Ltd.
Sydney, Australia
www.littlehills.com
lhills@bigpond.net.au
info@littlehills.com

Acknowledgements

All images © Little Hills Press except

Ian Read
55r, 60l

Colin Kerr
54

NorthernTerritory Tourist Commission
68-69, 73, 76, 77

Tourism Victoria
24-25, 35

Contents

New South Wales

Sydney, the capital city of New South Wales, is the birthplace of the Nation of Australia, and the largest city in the country. The state has breathtaking beaches and coastlines, cityscapes, World Heritage National Parks, snow-covered ski fields, and outback districts.

above Countryside near Goulburn in winter

CITY

Sydney was founded as a penal settlement,
but is now a thriving cosmopolitan metropolis.
Situated on a harbour that is arguably the most
beautiful in the world, the CBD is a bustling
area with shopping boutiques, dining and
entertainment venues, galleries, museums and
historic areas.

Sydney City
below

Sydney has come a long way since the days of Captain Phillip and the
First Fleet of 1788. From the Easern Suburbs, one has a panoramic view
of the Central Business District stretching from the Centrepoint Tower,
past the Renzo Piano designed Aurora Place to Circular Quay.

City
left
A view of the City over Farm Cove.

Sydney Harbour Bridge
The Bridge is one of Sydney's most famous landmarks. Completed in 1932, the construction of the bridge was an economic feat as well as an engineering triumph. Prior to its completion the only links between the city centre in the south and the residential north were by ferry, or by a 20 kilometre (12.5 miles) road route that involved five bridge crossings.

Sydney Opera House

Commenced in 1957 and completed in 1973, the Opera House is a unique building that has become the symbol of Sydney. It was designed to become part of its environment, and it doesn't take a lot of imagination to see it as something that could sail down the Harbour if it so desired. It has been listed as one of the world's premier attractions.

Taronga Zoo

Never before have people been able to experience all the wonders of the world's natural environments so close to the city. The Zoo's new precincts will immerse visitors in a natural and cultural experience.

Paddington

The streets of this inner city suburb are lined with pretty terrace houses that are decorated with `Paddington Lace', a distinctive wrought-iron trimming. Paddington hosts many antique shops, art galleries, and old-fashioned pubs

City Centre
near right

The city centre, with shops and eateries galore, has skyscrapers for a backdrop. It is a mecca for tourists from all over the world, as well as Sydneysiders out for lunch or in search of a bargain.

Cockle Bay, Darling Harbour

Innovative architecture is a feature of the Cockle Bay Wharf development, complemented by the space-age IMAX Theatre at its southern end. During lunchtimes and evenings, people stream from their offices to patronize the many cafes, bars and restaurants found along the trendy strip.

Department of Lands Building
far right

The classic edwardian sandstone building of the Department of Lands enhances Bridge Street. The statues of many local explorers grace the facade.

Hyde Park

left

The Archibald Fountain, with its fanning peacock-pattern spray, captures the attention of people strolling through the north section of Hyde Park. The south section is home to the War Memorial; the western boundary adjoins the commerce and trade district of Market and Elizabeth Streets; and the eastern boundary leads to St Mary's Cathedral.

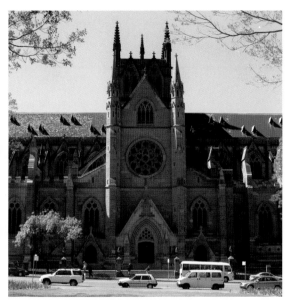

St Mary's Cathedral

Built in the Gothic Revival style, St Mary's is the legacy of a 62-year project completed in 1928. Vaulted ceilings, intricate statues, period-piece gargoyles and crafted side altars, make the church interior both beautiful and fascinating. Outstanding stained glass windows depict scenes in the life of the Blessed Virgin Mary, and of the early days of the Catholic Church.

Sydney Tower

right

The Tower reaches high into the sky above the Centrepoint Shopping Centre, which is known as the `Heart of the City'.

COASTAL

New South Wales is well-known for its beautiful coasts and bays that stretch for 350 kilometres. The beaches boasts of dazzling white sand and surfing waters.

Batemans Bay
right

A popular weekend and holiday retreat, especially for those from Canberra. Well-known for its 16 golden beaches, the Clyde River and its superb fishing. This is the only town that permits commercial fishing trawlers to sell their catch to the public.

Wollongong from Mt Kembla

Famed for its wonderful surfing beaches and busy steelworks, the city also has many sporting facilities, and an extensive botanic garden adjacent to a well regarded university (left foreground). As with many major shipping ports, a lighthouse stands sentinel over the city and harbour.

Coogee Beach

Affectionately known as `Sydney's Seaside Village', with many of its
streets still using their original sea creature's names, Coogee is a popular
destination for locals and tourists attracted to its beach and its very
popular Coogee Bay Hotel.

Ulladulla Beach

Ulladulla Beach, on the New South Wales south coast, is a tranquil setting most of the year. However, the summer holiday months see thousands of people flock here from the inland and from the north. Australia's coastline is mostly blessed with white, soft, sandy beaches.

Byron Bay Area

top right

This north coast area boasts great surfing beaches and a subtropical climate. Byron has been a mecca for a myriad of people, from backpackers and bohemians, to more conservative types.

Bondi Beach

bottom right

Bondi is Sydney's most famous beach, and people from all over the city flock there on summer days to stake their claim to a golden patch of sand. Inviting water temperature, and the safety provided by an elite surf lifesaving team add to the beach's popularity.

NEW SOUTH WALES
INLAND

Although the majority of Australia's population is cluttered around the coastline, there are many inland districts that are popular as alternative and more affordable residences. One example is the Blue Mountains area, to the west of Sydney.

Blue Mountains

Katoomba is approximately 110 kilometres from central Sydney, and around 1000 metres (3336 feet) above sea level. It encompasses Echo Point which give views to Mount Solitary (left) and the Three Sisters. Winters here are chilly and summers are mild, while February has the most rainfall.

Echo Point *(top left)*

The lookout at Echo Point offers extensive views of the thickly wooded Blue Mountains, including the famous Three Sisters (above), a popular trio that is important in Aboriginal legends. Throughout the mountains the creeks and fault lines are reflected in the indentations in the vegetation.

Bathurst Orange Area

Typical New South Wales countryside beyond the Great Dividing Range. This land provides for vineyards, grain crops, sheep and cattle.

Little Hills

left

Little Hills and Murrurundi, as seen from the pass on the Crown of the Liverpool Range.

The Blue Mountains

far left

In autumn the Blue Mountains are alive with trees of bright reds, oranges and browns. The mountains are dotted with many small towns that have roadside stalls offering fresh fruit and vegetables.

Thredbo Creek

The Thredbo River meanders through the heart of beautiful Kosciusko National Park. This area is a playground for skiers during the winter months, and for bushwalkers at other times.

Church at Perisher

Perisher, in the Snowy Mountains, is one of the ski fields of New South Wales.

Victoria

above Melboure City Centre

Victoria, the Garden State, is situated in the south-eastern corner of Australia, and well known for its acres of parklands along the Yarra River, its tree-lined boulevards, and extensive gardens. Though Victoria is the second smallest state in the country, it is rich in culture with many festivals. Attractions include wineries, lakes, mountains, landscapes and native wildlife.

CITY

Melbourne is the capital of Victoria, and is located on the shores of Port Phillip Bay with the Yarra River flowing through the city centre. Stylish and elegant, Melbourne is known as the Fashion Capital of Australia, and is recognized for its interest in the arts, fine food, wine and shopping.

Princes Bridge

below

This is one of Melbourne's oldest and grandest bridges, and is located at the point where Swanston Street becomes St Kilda Road. Built around 1886, it replaced an old wooden bridge that had been opened by Lieutenant-Governor La Trobe in 1850.

Trams

near right

Trams are just about the `symbol' of Melbourne, and are a big draw-card for visitors who are provided with an interesting, reliable and efficient way to get around the city. These vehicles, some old-fashioned and some sleek and modern, continue to provide transport for thousands of commuters.

Flinders Station

far right

The end of Elizabeth Street comes alive at night with the lights illuminating the grand Flinders Street Station.

Collins Street

above

A fashion boutique mecca of designer labels and specialty shops. Linked to Bourke and Little Collins Streets, these arcades are solely dedicated to those who seek some serious retail therapy.

CBD
far left
A real Melbourne icon, the Rialto Towers Building stands 253 metres (830 feet) high. The Observation Deck has breathtaking views of the city and surrounding areas.

Kings Domain, Melbourne
above
South of the Yarra River, many gardens surrounds St Kilda Road and gives a wonderful aspect to this part of the city. The Kings Domain is part of this setting.

COAST

Travelling along the Victorian coastline guarantees stunning ocean views, laid-back coastal towns and villages. The contours of the rocky and jagged south-west coast offer opportunities to soak up the sun and water, fish or whale watch.

The Twelve Apostles

below

The Great Ocean Road travels along the southern coastline and provides spectacular views of rugged rock formations that have been formed by the stormy nature of the Southern Ocean.

Loch Ard Gorge

above

Visitors to the Gorge are treated to a beautiful vista of towering cliffs, sparkling blue-green sea and a small, sandy beach. It is hard to imagine that the drama of one of Victoria's most tragic shipwrecks was played out at this very spot, giving its name to the gorge.

Port Phillip Bay

right, below

Sunset on Port Phillip Bay, viewed from Edithvale south of Mordialloc. The beaches on the eastern shores of the Bay have beautiful white sands, but no surf. This is an idyllic place for a stroll in the evening.

INLAND

Victoria's inland is natural sheep grazing country, complimented by fruit orchards, vineyards, caves and mountains, heritage buildings, mining towns and abandoned gold mine.

Floating Islands

This is an eerie vision west of Colac at Pirron Yallock. Masses of peat have become detached from their bases to float over the lake, and so the area is called the Floating Islands National Park.

Bogong High Plains

above, below

Mt Bogong, Victoria's highest peak, sits at 1986m (6516 feet) above sea level, providing wonderful views of Mt Feathertop and the western peaks.

Mount Arapiles

Mount Arapiles rises sharply from the Wimmera plains to form part of the Mount Arapiles-Tooan State Park. The park includes Mitre Rock, the Tooan block and examples of about 14 per cent of the state's flora species.

Grampians

Victoria's largest National Park and the southern most extremity of the Great Dividing Range, these picturesque mountains are comprised of outstanding landforms, dense rainforests, unsurpassed mountain peaks, sparkling waterfalls and superb lookouts. The area abounds with fauna and flora as well as Aboriginal rock art sites.

Lake View

A view of the lake in the Bogong National Park.

McKenzie Falls

right

McKenzie Falls is the largest and most popular of the many waterfalls in The Grampians.

Country Victoria

left

Victoria is home to large tracts of lush greenery, trickling creeks and majestic mountain views. There are many areas that are perfect for picnics, bushwalks, wildlife observation, and day trips.

Tasmania

Australia's only island state, Tasmania can boasts world heritage buildings, relics of its convict past, orchards and vineyards, national parks, rugged mountains, rolling green hills and raging rivers. The extinct Tasmanian Tiger once roamed throughout the state.

above Inland Tasman countryside

TASMANIA

CITY

Hobart is the capital of Tasmania, and the second oldest city of Australia. It lies between the Derwent River Estuary at Stormy Bay and the foot of Mount Wellington. Its architecture is a reflection of its age.

Hobart
below

A view of the city and its environs from Mount Wellington, highlighting the Tasman Bridge and the Derwent River.

Hobart

top

Fishing vessels moor in this area of the port of Hobart as do ocean going vessels. It also is home to many sailing yachts that compete in the Sydney to Hobart race in late December every year. The north side of the dock is lined by National Trust-listed warehouses that are still in use today.

Mersey River, Devonport

above

Thousands of visitors disembark from the Spirit of Tasmania at the port of Devonport, which is the fourth largest city in Tasmania. It was originally made up of two towns, Formby and Torquay, however they voted to consolidate in 1893.

TASMANIA
INLAND

Tasmania is known for its tranquil forests and mountain ranges, and old historical towns with beautifully preserved buildings.

Derwent River

above

A view of the Derwent River at New Norfolk, 70 kilometres (44 miles) west of Hobart.

Mount Field National Park

This is a scene of tropical vegetation in an unlikely place. The base of Mount Field National Park is home to Russell Falls and lush vegetation that extends up the valley to the Falls. These are easily accessible by foot, and are close to the entrance to the Park, which is about 80 kilometres (50 miles) from Hobart.

Mount Roland

Though the mountains in Australia are not high (Australia's highest mountain, Mt Kosciusko, is 2230 metres - 7314 feet), they tend to dominate the landscape.

Devils Gullet

Devils Gullet State Reserve is 40 kilometres (25 miles) from Mole Creek, in one of
Tasmania's United Nations World Heritage Areas. The Devils Gullet lookout stands atop
a 600 metre (1800 feet) sheer cliff, and provides amazing 180-degree views of the Fisher
River Valley. Part of the road to the lookout is unsealed and makes for slow going, but even
the views from the road are attractive.

Derwent Valley

Sheep graze in the Derwent Valley, inland from Hobart. The area is better known for its apples and hops (see the Oast House, where the hops are dried, in the background).

COAST

The Tasmanian coast is full of many contrasts. In the west, the roaring forties lash an almost inaccessible coastline, creating a forbidding landscape. On the other hand, the east coast boasts tranquil bays, white sandy beaches, accessible offshore islands and wonderful surf throughout the summer.

Convict Prison, Port Arthur

Governor George Arthur first established a prison at Port Arthur in 1830. The prison was built 100 kilometres (60 miles) from Hobart, on a peninsula that was reached by a narrow stretch of land named Eaglehawk Neck. It was an easy place to guard with soldiers and dogs. Closed in the 1880s, it had a history as a harsh institution for multiple offenders and political prisoners. Now it's a peaceful settlement amidst english oaks and expansive green lawns.

Freycinet National Park
above

The pink granite cliffs and dazzling blue sea are captured here in the muted tones of an early morning winter chill.

Tasman Peninsula
left

Looking south from the Devil's Kitchen and Tasman Arch; The cliff faced shoreline with its rock platforms is typical of the area. These formations are interspersed with protected bays.

Freycinet National Park

left

From within Freycinet National Park, this view across Coles Bay looks towards the main part of the island near Swansea on the east coast of Tasmania. Illuminated by midday light, the rich colours of the outcrop reach towards the faint coastline in the distance. Thick, sugar-white clouds fill a slice of Australian sky.

Sandy Bay Marina

above

Yachts remain at anchor in a delightful part of Hobart. In the background is the historical area of Battery Point.

South Australia

South Australia is renowned for its vineyards, and produces seventy per cent of Australian wines, most of which are exported. It comes as no surprise then that it is known as the Wine State. Features of South Australia include the Outback and the sea, and there are many festivals and cultural activities.

CITY

Adelaide, the capital of South Australia, is known as the City of Churches. It is a well-planned city with many restored colonial buildings, and many parks and gardens.

Adelaide

The River Torrens flows through the centre of the city, which lies on a narrow coastal plain bounded on the west by the Gulf of St Vincent and on the east by the Mount Lofty Ranges. A view of the city from the ranges (left).

SOUTH AUSTRALIA
COAST

The South Australian coast has some areas that offer attractive and enticing beaches; some that are interlaced with mangrove mudflats; and others where the raging ocean waters and rugged rocks discourage visitors.

Great Australian Bight

The Bight is well known as a crucial calving area for the Southern Right Whale, but it also provides a vital habitat for the endangered Australian Sea Lion, as well as other types of sea creatures (eg. great white sharks, scores of fish and other whale types).

INLAND

The South Australian inland is an ensemble of hills, gorges, valleys, vineyards and mountains.

Homestead
below
The old Post and Telegraph Station at Willunga township.

Naracoorte Caves

Situated in the south-east corner of South Australia, the stalagmite and stalactite formations in Naracoorte Caves are part of the National Park 12 kilometres (7 miles) south-east of Penola. There are some 60 known caves along a 25 kilometre (15 mile) range.

Mt Bayley
This is one of the 75 old mining areas in the Flinders Ranges.

Clare Valley
left

The Clare Valley is one of the most famous wine producing areas in Australia. First inhabited by settlers from England, Ireland and Poland in the 1800's, a rich heritage of both villages and architecture can be observed in the area. The wide variety of excellent local wineries can also be visited.

Western Australia

above The Pinnacles

Australia's biggest state, Western Australia covers a third of the island continent. It is larger than the whole of Western Europe, and four times the size of Texas, USA. The eastern border is a hot red desert, while the western border is hundreds of kilometres of beautiful coastline.

WESTERN AUSTRALIA
CITY

The capital of Western Australia is Perth, the city of the millionaires. The sunniest of all Australian cities, it has on average eight hours of sun each day. Perth nestles by a kilometre-wide expanse of the Swan River, and is edged by expensive suburbs and white sandy beaches.

Scuptures in front of the Western Australian Library

above

Sculptured forms stand sentinel at the entrance to the Library. This area to the east of the city centre also houses the State Art Gallery and the Museum.

Swan Bells Tower

right

The Swan Bells include the twelve bells of St Martin-in-the-Fields, in existence since the late 13th century, and six new bells. The tower was built to house all 18 bells and to re-commemorate and re-celebrate many historic events. The bells are rung at regular intervals.

Alf Curlewis Gardens
above
The Gardens overlook the modern skyscrapers of Perth whilst facing the river banks on the other side.

Central Railway Station, Wellington St
left
Now known as Perth Train Station, it was built between 1893 and 1894, and replaced an earlier station that was built in 1881.

WESTERN AUSTRALIA
INLAND

Going inland into Western Australia offers the chance of exploring wilderness areas, mountain ranges, world renowned vineyards, forests, rivers, mining towns, caves, national parks, deserts and seemingly unending paddocks of wheat.

Ashburton River

The Ashburton flows 560 kilometres (348 miles) inland in the north-west region of Western Australia, and is the main river system in the Ashburton River Basin. It has a number of smaller rivers and creeks branching from the main channel. Its floodplains are mostly flat, wide and sediment filled, flowing only after seasonal rainfall or cyclone activity.

Gum Trees

right

This is a study of typical Australian foliage, the gum tree, windblown and scraggy, but still there.

One of many old buildings in New Norcia

above

Home to Benedictine Monks, this heritage site was founded by Dom Rosendo Salvado in 1846. Developed in the cleric Benedictine style of self-sufficient community, the abbey did much for the aboriginal tribes in the area, serving them for some one hundred and fifty years. Today it is an education, tourist and spiritual renewal centre.

Paddy Hannan Sculpture, Burswood Park

left

Paddy Hannan, who discovered gold near Kalgoorlie in 1893, pushes his wheelbarrow beside the Great Eastern Highway, and glances over his shoulder at the traffic heading east towards his beloved Goldfields. The sculptures at Burswood Park pay homage to the thousands of forgotten men who came to Western Australia in search of their fortunes.

Pinnacles
These unusual rock formations are found in the Red Desert area of the Nambung National Park on the coast of Western Australia, about two and a half hours north of Perth.

On the road to Moora
above
A dynamic wheat producing area north west of Perth

WESTERN AUSTRALIA
COAST

The Western Australian coast stretches for miles on end, tracing the contours of half the country. It is recognized for its surfing beaches, islands, picturesque scenery and some rugged stretches.

Prevelly Beach
top right
A pristine beach popular with surfers

Margaret River
bottom right
The Margaret River region is a rich dairy, cattle and timber region, but is better known Australia-wide for its production of excellent wines. It is also a popular holiday destination offering swimming, fishing and surfing. The Mammoth and Lake Caves are nearby.

Busselton Jetty, Busselton
above
The wooden jetty is over two kilometres in length and was restored after being damaged by Cyclone Alby in 1978.

Cape Naturaliste Lighthouse, Yallingup

far left

The lighthouse overlooking Geographe Bay, once home to many whaling ships, was constructed in 1903 from local limestone. It continues to guide shipping off the west coast. The unspoiled bays in this region of the south-west provide safe swimming and fishing, thanks to the protection of the cape.

Eagle Bay

left, above

Northern Territory

above The Devil's Marbles

The Territory covers one-sixth of Australia, and is divided into two regions, the Top End and the Red Centre. The Top End encapsulates the city of Darwin and its rugged coasts, whilst the Red Centre is home to the monolith Uluru (Ayres Rock), the 36 domes of Kata Tjuta (The Olgas) and the famous town of Alice Springs. This is true Outback country.

NORTHERN TERRITORY
INLAND

The inland is a blend of mining towns, furrowed land, square kilometres of bushland, national parks, unremitting desert, appeasing lagoons, and an abundance of Aboriginal culture.

Rock Paintings

The ancient rock paintings at Obiri Rock in the Kakadu National Park are a record of essential aspects of the culture of the Aboriginal tribe of the area.

Salt Water Crocodiles
Danger lurks around every corner in the Top End. Fifteen metre
Saltwater Crocs are famous for their ferocious jaws.

Kangaroos
One of the highly recognized
symbols of Australia is the native
Kangaroo. The grey and red
Kangaroos belong to the same
family.

Victoria River in Gregory National Park

This area is ranked as one of the most beautiful and dramatic in the Territory. It has rugged cliffs, attractive gorges and huge natural amphitheatres.

Katherine Gorge

left

Katherine Gorge is located in Nitmiluk National Park. The National Park is rich in Aboriginal art, with rock paintings representing the spiritual `dreaming' of the Jawoyn people, the traditional owners of the land.

Kakadu National Park

Comprising 8000 square miles of spectacular wildlife habitat, the Kakadu National Park has a range of high stone, plateau, forest woodland and monsoon rainforest. There are open savanna-like flood plains with billabongs, mangrove-fringed estuaries, plus the coastal beaches of the Arafura Sea.

Uluru (Ayers Rock)

An amazing monolith in the middle of the Australian continent (465 kilometres - 290 miles - south-west of Alice Springs) on a flat plain of spinifex and other grasses. The traditional owners are the Anangu (Pitjantjatjara and Yantunytjatjara people) a number of whom live in the nearby Mutiljulu Community.

Mount Connor

top right

Mount Connor is a sprawling sandstone mesa about 90 kilometres (56 miles) east of Uluru. It is part of the Curtain Springs property, it can be climbed on the south side. The mount changes colours from soft pinks to dusky reds, depending on the time of day and year.

Kata Tjuta (Mt Olga)

bottom right

Just 48 kilometres (30 miles) west of Uluru, and standing some 200 metres taller, are 36 individual domes known to the Anangu as Kata Tjuta — the place of many heads. This is a collection of giant weathered red domes with fissures, gorges and valleys carved between them, that are home to some captivating creatures of the region, such as the reptile the Thorny Devil.

NORTHERN TERRITORY
CITY

Previously known as Stuart, the city of Alice Springs is the second largest town of the Northern Territory. It lies at the foot of the picturesque MacDonnell Ranges, in the geographic centre of the Australian Continent.

Alice Springs

With a population of 30,000, Alice Springs is Australia's premier Outback town. Some 1500 kilometres (932 miles) south of Darwin, and surrounded by ancient ranges and red desert, *The Alice* is now a modern city with a good shopping centre, very comfortable accommodation, and a good selection of entertainment venues. Everyone looks forward to the annual Henley on Todd, the only dry river regatta in the world.

NORTHERN TERRITORY
COAST

The northern coastline, mostly unspoiled, is sprawled with stretches of mangroves that cover one third of its coast, rocky headlands, pristine sandy beaches and remote reef systems.

Darwin

The relaxed capital of the Northern Territory is Darwin, a city of 109,419 people, located on Australia's far north-western coastline. It was a strategic outpost during World War II, and suffered tremendous damage during 64 air raids, with the loss of 243 lives. On Christmas Eve in 1974, Darwin was struck by one of the greatest natural disasters in Australian history, Cyclone Tracy, which left only approximately 500 of the city's then 8000 homes habitable.

Queensland

above Brisbane from the Brisbane River

Queensland, as the travel brochures say, is `beautiful one day, perfect the next'. A true tropical paradise, the state offers beautiful beaches, verdant rainforests, the stunning Outback, vibrant cities and a myriad of attractions. It is known as the Sunshine State.

QUEENSLAND
CITY

The capital of Queensland is Brisbane, which is situated on the banks of the Brisbane River. It boasts a sub-tropical climate and a very relaxed lifestyle.

Brisbane Parliament House
right

It was built in the settlement period and exhibits Renaissance style aesthetics. The building overlooks the Botanic Gardens.

Story Bridge
top right

The Story Bridge was Brisbane's answer to the Sydney Harbour Bridge. Built during the depression of the 1930s, it gave much needed work to many of the unemployed.

Captain Cook Bridge
bottom right

Flowing through the city, the Brisbane River is spanned by five bridges, all of which have their own unique style of architecture. The Captain Cook Bridge was built in 1972, and connects central Brisbane to Wooloongabba. It is majestic in size and looks its best at night.

INLAND

Inland Queensland is home to a fusion of true Outback country and dry bushlands on the one hand, and lush rainforests and mountain ranges on the other.

Windmill

right

Sunset in Outback Australia. The windmill driving the bore water to the surface is a symbol of the Outback and a water feature in an otherwise arid landscape.

Stockyard

Manning the gates of a stockyard in northern Queensland. The cattle industry is one of Australia's most important export earners.

Sugarcane Fields

Over 68,000 hectares of land are used for the cultivation of sugar cane in the Hinchinbrook Shire. A small proportion of the land is irrigated, with the growers relying primarily on rain-fed irrigation. The natural tropical conditions provide the ability to produce high yielding crops of sugar cane.

Sugar Cane Burning

North of Mackay, this now outmoded technique of burning off before harvesting sugar cane is, if nothing else, a spectacular sight.

QUEENSLAND
COAST

The Queensland Coast consists of hundreds of pristine sandy white beaches, coral reefs and an abundance of sun.

Shute Harbour
below

Young explorers scavenge among rock pools on the sunny harbour. Mangrove trees are a familiar site in these parts of the coast.

Shute Harbour

above

The Harbour is a point of departure for many vessels cruising the Whitsunday Islands, and the second busiest passenger port in the country.

Great Barrier Reef

The famous reef lies on the coastal edges of Northern Queensland. Beginning at Breaksea Spit, north of Bundaberg, it extends 2030 kilometres (1260 miles) north to the waters of New Guinea, making it the longest series of coral reefs and islands in the world. The reef is home to vast numbers of colourful species of fish and numerous varieties of corals.

Sunshine Coast
left, above left

The Sunshine Coast stretches from Caloundra, north of Brisbane, to Double Island Point in the north. It boasts of 55 kilometres (34 miles) of white sandy beaches,such as Noosa (above left), rocky headlands and sugarcane farms(left).

Sunset at Glass House Mountains
above

These sentinel-like figures are of historic value to Aboriginals. Located inland from the Sunshine Coast.

Australian Capital Territory

Established in 1911, the independent capital territory was created out of political necessity free from domination by any one state. Gardens and parks surround the city.

above From Mount Ainslie looking down Anzac Parade to the Australian Parliament. This strip is regarded symbolically as the core of the nation.

AUSTRALIAN CAPITAL TERRITORY
CITY

Canberra is Australia's national capital, founded in 1913. In concept it is a garden city surrounded with a variation of shades and colours. It is the home of the Commonwealth Parliament.

Lake Burley Griffin
Formed in 1963 and named after Canberra's designer, American architect Walter Burley Griffin. Over 400 hectares of parkland have been developed around 35 kilometres (22 miles) of foreshore.

Telstra Tower
The Telstra Tower on Black Mountain dominates the Canberra Skyline. It houses a viewing platform, various communication facilities, a kiosk and a revolving restaurant that affords magnificent views of the surrounding countryside.

Parliament House
above

Parliament House, in keeping with Walter Burley Griffin's original plan, is the central landmark of Canberra. While some might not be taken with the 81 metre (266 feet) stainless steel flagpole that dominates the city, all have to agree that the interior of the building is magnificent.

Old Parliament Building
top

The building was home to Australia's Federal Parliament from 1927 to 1988. It is now a nationally significant heritage site housing various exhibitions.

War Memorial, Canberra

above

The centre of the ceiling of the shrine in the Australian War Memorial, Canberra.

War Memorial, Canberra

right

An aspect of the surrounds of the Australian War Memorial, with relics from earlier conflicts.

War Memorial, Canberra

Stained glass window in the interior of the centre of the Australian War Memorial in Canberra. The memorial honours all those who served in all conflicts in which Australia has been involved, and especially those who made the supreme sacrifice.

INDEX

NORTHERN
TERRITORY

QUEENSLAND

WESTERN
AUSTRALIA

SOUTH
AUSTRALIA

NEW SOUTH
WALES

ACT

VICTORIA

TASMANIA